Our Aim

Rook Publishing is committed to rediscovering historic, rare, and out-of-print books, and ensuring that such literary works are reproduced so that they may be preserved for future generations.

Preserving the Past

Because we consider this work to have significant historic and cultural importance, we have made it available as part of our commitment to protect and preserve the world's literature in affordable, high quality, modern reproductions that remain true to the original work

This book is a facsimile reprint of a scarce and antiquarian book. Due the age and source of the original document, it may contain imperfections such as notations, marginalia, marks and other flaws within its pages.

www.rookpublishing.co.uk

RITUAL

AND

BOOK *of* FORMS

FOR

SUBORDINATE LODGES

OF THE

AMERICAN ORDER.
SONS OF ST. GEORGE

As revised and rewritten from former Rituals, by a Committee composed of George T. Watts, George Tucker, William J. Abbotts, John Chorley, A. P. Marsh, Robert W. Cooper, and John Bramwell, appointed at the Supreme Lodge Session at Pittsburg, Pa., 1928, and adopted by the Supreme Lodge in session at Niagara Falls, N. Y., October 7, 1931.

Printed by

KEYSTONE PRINT, INC.

Brockton, Mass.

Officers of Subordinate Lodges

JUNIOR PAST PRESIDENT

PRESIDENT

VICE-PRESIDENT

SECRETARY

TREASURER

MESSENGER

ASSISTANT SECRETARY

ASSISTANT MESSENGER

CHAPLAIN

INSIDE SENTINEL

OUTSIDE SENTINEL

THREE TRUSTEES

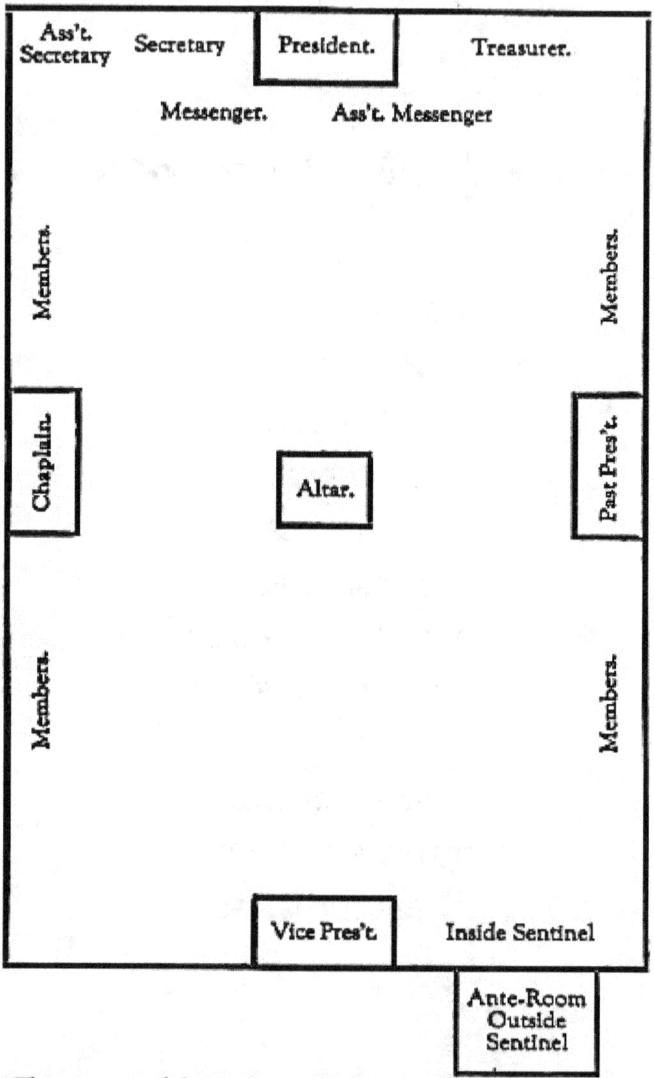

Ass't.
Secretary   Secretary   President.   Treasurer.

Messenger.   Ass't. Messenger

Members.   Members.

Chaplain.   Altar.   Past Pres't.

Members.   Members.

Vice Pres't.   Inside Sentinel

Ante-Room
Outside
Sentinel

"The position of the Secretary, Treasurer and Assistant Secretary,
may be changed to suit the will of the Lodge."

Ceremonies of
OPENING and CLOSING
and
ORDER of BUSINESS

θ   θ   θ   θ   θ   θ

OPENING OF LODGE

W. P.—Officers and Brothers: Clothe your-
selves in regalia. Officers take your stations.
Worthy Inside Sentinel, notify Brothers in the
ante-room to enter, secure the door, and allow no
Brother to enter until I declare this Lodge regularly open.

*(Worthy Inside Sentinel admits Brothers, closes inner
door and returns to station.)*

W. I. S.—Worthy President, I have secured the
inner door.

W. P.—Worthy Messengers: (Messengers rise
and face the W. P.) Advance and give me the current password. (Messengers advance, give password to W. P. and return to stations facing W. P.)
Proceed on the right and left, see that all present
have on their regalia, and are in possession of the
password; if not, immediately report to the Past
Worthy President.

(Worthy Messengers return to stations, facing the W. P.)

W. M.—Worthy President, I find the Brothers on your right are in possession of the password and have on their regalia.

W. A. M.—Worthy President, I find the Brothers on your left are in possession of the password and have on their regalia.

(Messengers face altar.)
(Call up officers.)

W. P.—Worthy Inside Sentinel, direct the Worthy Outside Sentinel to present himself, and you remain in his station until relieved.

(W. I. S. and W. O. S. change stations.)

W. O. S.—Worthy President, I report for instruction.

W. P.—Worthy Outside Sentinel, your duty is to guard the outer door; upon you depends the privacy of this Lodge. Return to your station and relieve the Worthy Inside Sentinel.

(After W. I. S. returns to his station, the Worthy President proceeds.)

W. P.—Past Worthy President, what are the duties of your office?

P. W. P.—It is my duty to pass upon the right of all Brothers to remain in, or be admitted to the Lodge.

W. P.—Worthy Vice-President, what are the duties of your office?

W. V. P.—It is my duty to perform the ceremonies intrusted to me; support the Worthy President in the discharge of his duties; assist him in maintaining order in the Lodge room; and appoint a minority of all committees unless otherwise ordered by the Lodge.

W. P.—Worthy Secretary, what are the duties of your office?

W. S.—It is my duty to keep a true and accurate account between the Lodge and its Members; receive all moneys and pay the same over to the Worthy Treasurer, taking his receipt therefor; attend to all the correspondence of the Lodge; and, in conjunction with the Worthy Assistant Secretary, keep a true and complete record of all the proceedings of this Lodge.

W. P.—Worthy Messenger, what are the duties of your office?

W. M.—It is my duty to examine the Brothers prior to the opening of the Lodge; assist the Worthy President as he may direct; prepare the Lodge room for the meetings of the Lodge; and see that all Lodge properties are collected at the close of each meeting.

W. P.—Worthy Inside Sentinel, what are the duties of your office?

W. I. S.—It is my duty to admit every Brother in possession of the password, or inform the Past

Worthy President that the Brother wishing to enter is without the password, and await his commands.

(Call up.)

W. P.—Worthy Chaplain, you will please lead us in prayer.

W. C.—Let us pray.

W. P.—Officers and Brothers, all unite in singing our Opening Ode.

Opening Ode.

Tune, "Duke Street." — J. HATTON.

W. P.—Officers and Brothers: It is my duty to open this Lodge for the transaction of such business as may be in order and properly brought before it. While we are together let no animosity hold an influence over our hearts, no unseemly conduct mar the pleasure of our meeting. Unity of opinion cannot be expected on all subjects, but the harmony of this Lodge will not be disturbed if the members will submit to the will of the majority. These principles and motives actuating us, we shall not fail in our objects—the advancement of our Order, and the welfare of all worthy Brothers.

FLOOR WORK INSTRUCTIONS

Opening and Closing Ceremonies

Note: The Bible, Sword and Shield are placed on altar, in position indicated per diagram, prior to opening ceremony.

W. P.—Worthy Messengers and Worthy Chaplain.

(Messengers and Chaplain arise and face Worthy President. Messengers draw, present and then carry swords.)

W. P.—Adjust the altar.

(Messengers again present and carry swords, right about face and proceed with the Worthy Chaplain per diagram, stopping three paces from altar.

Messengers present and sheathe swords.

Worthy Messenger advances to altar, removes and places shield on left forearm at position to defend body, then steps back to his position in line.

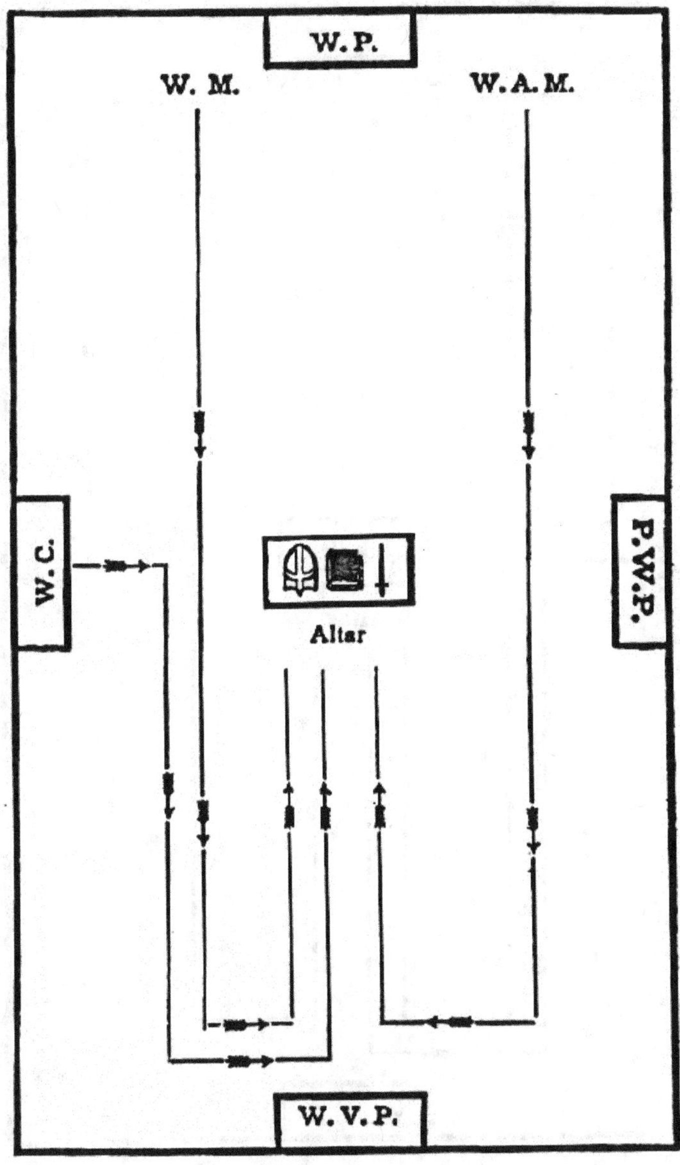

W. P.
W. M.
W. A. M.
W. C.
P.W.P.
Altar
W. V. P.

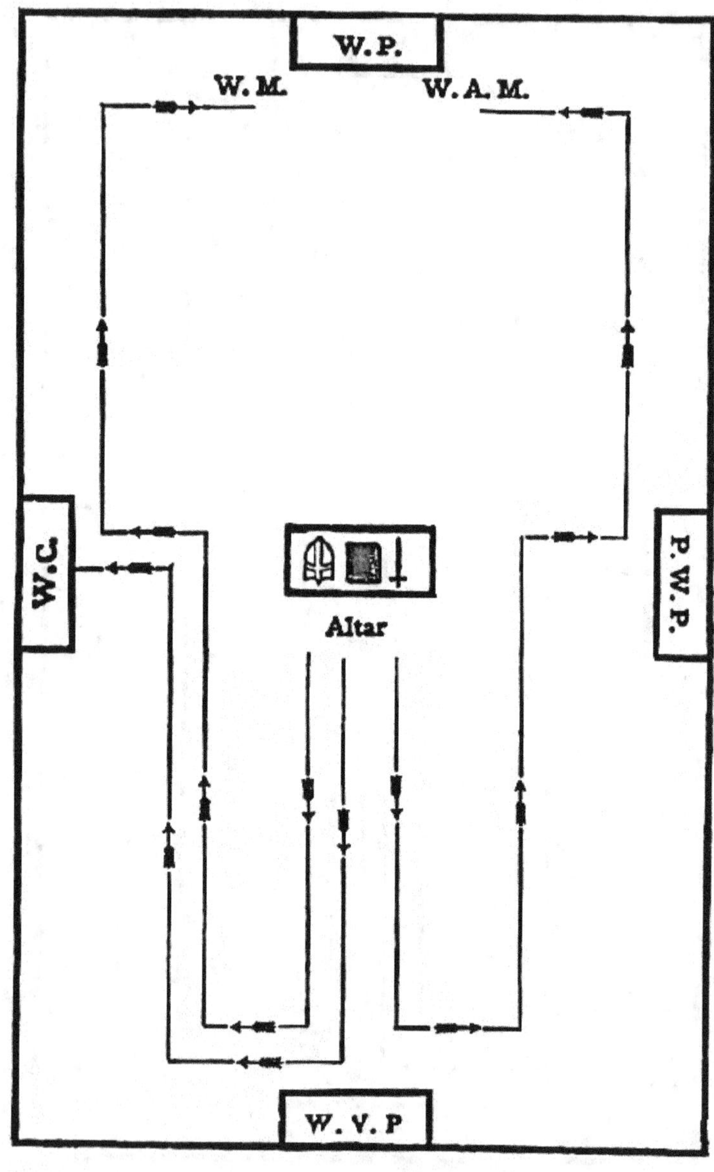

W.P.
W. M.
W. A. M.
W.C
P.W.P.
Altar
W. V. P

Worthy Assistant Messenger advances to altar, removes and presents sword, then to position carry; then steps back to his position in line.

Worthy Chaplain advances to altar, opens and places Bible in proper position, then steps back to his position in line.

Worthy Messenger advances and places shield in proper position, then steps back to his position.

Worthy Assistant Messenger then advances, places sword in proper position, then steps back to his position.)

(After the altar has been adjusted the W. P. will say.)

W. P.—Officers and Brothers, by virtue of the power invested in me as Worthy President, I declare the Lodge legally open.

(Messengers and Chaplain approach altar and salute, right about face and then return to their stations.)

(Note: In closing, the same procedure is carried out; leaving the Bible, Sword and Shield in the same position on the altar as prior to opening ceremony. No member should pass between the altar and dais of the W. P. while the altar is adjusted.)
(Call down.)

W. P.—Worthy Inside Sentinel, admit any Brother wishing to enter.

ORDER OF BUSINESS

W. P.—Worthy Secretary or the Worthy Assistant Secretary, call the roll of officers. (Worthy Messenger rises and answers roll.)

W. P.—Worthy Secretary or the Worthy Assistant Secretary, read the minutes of our preceding meeting.

W. P.—Brothers, the minutes just read are minutes of our last regular meeting. Is there anything omitted, or are there any corrections to be made? (Pause.) If not I declare them approved as read. (Should there be any corrections made,) I declare them approved as corrected.

W. P.—Report of the Relief Committee and reading of sick claims and certificates.

W. P.—Report of Investigating Committee.

(The reports from the Investigating Committees must be read by the Worthy Secretary and if reported favorably by Committee and Physician, be balloted for. If no reports, omit the form of balloting and continue with reports of committees, page 15.)

W. P.—Worthy Messenger, prepare the ballot box.

(When prepared it must be inspected by the W. P. and W. V. P. then be placed on the altar.)

(The Messenger and Asst. Messenger will stand one on each side of the altar, four paces back, allowing only one Brother to advance to the ballot box at a time. At least seven ballots must be cast to constitute a legal election.)

W. P.—Brothers, you will cast your ballot for Mr........., for initiation into this Lodge. He has been favorably reported upon by the Committee and Physician. Form in single file in front of the altar. facing the dais. White balls elect; three black balls or cubes reject. Take due care and avoid errors. I now declare the ballot open.

W. P.—Have all voted who wish? If so, I declare the ballot closed. Worthy Messenger, display the ballot box to the Worthy Vice-President, then bring it to me for inspection.

W. P.—Worthy Vice-President, how find you the ballot?

W. V. P.—Favorable (or unfavorable) to the candidate.

W. P.—Favorable (or unfavorable) here. I therefore declare Mr.........duly elected for initiation into this Lodge.

(If the ballot is unfavorable another ballot must be taken, if still unfavorable the applicant must be declared rejected.)

(If there are candidates to be initiated, they may be initiated at this, or any time, during Lodge session. For ceremony of initiation, see Page No. 18.)

W. P.—Reports of Committees by seniority.

W. P.—Does any member know of a Brother sick or in distress?

W. P.—Proposals for membership.

W. P.—Communications.

W. P.—Payment of bills.

W. P.—Unfinished business.

W. P.—There will be a recess of five minutes for the payment of dues.

W. P.—New business.

W. P.—Receipts of the evening.

W. P.—Good and welfare.

(Under this heading subjects for the benefit of the Order may be discussed or social and entertaining features introduced, but business requiring a vote of the Lodge cannot be entertained under this head.)

CLOSING

W. P.—Officers and Brothers, all unite in singing our CLOSING ODE.

W. P.—Worthy Messengers and Worthy Chaplain (W. Ms. and W. C. rise and face the W. P.), dismantle the altar and when the Lodge is closed the Worthy Messengers will be careful to collect all Lodge property. (The W. Ms. and W. C. will return to their stations and the W. P. will say,)

W. P.—Officers and Brothers, I now declare this Lodge closed, and bid you to retire in Faith, Hope and Love, Faith in our principles, Hope in our Future, and Love for our cause.

Closing Ode.

Tune, "Auld Lang Syne."

1. And now, the hour once more has come When, Brothers, we must part;
2. 'Till link'd fast by the gold-en chain Of love and sympathy,

Let us re-mem-ber, ev-'ry one, The cause we have at heart.
A might-y band of Brotherhood, St. GEORGE'S SONS will be.

God pros-per still our glorious cause, And bless the grand design,
Thus, as we give our parting word, Once more our vows we plight,

Till Brit-ons, in fra-ter-nal love, Their hands together join.
To live in peace and har-mo-ny—Good night, good night, good night!

The American Order, Sons of St. George

CEREMONY OF INITIATION

Instructions and Suggestions

Under extraordinary circumstances, when a candidate must be initiated hurriedly, the following method may be used. The candidate will be admitted by the W. M. in the proper form, and, after the candidate has answered affirmatively that he is willing to take the obligation, the W. P. will direct the W. M. to place the candidate in position at the altar to receive the obligation. Following the obligation the W. M. will present the candidate to the W. P. who will give him the signs, grips and password. He will conclude by signing the constitution. It is essential that the candidate receive the lectures at some future date.

To make the initiatory degree as effective and instructive as possible, each officer is expected to commit his lecture or charge to memory.

Lodges are at liberty to allow their degree teams to use soloists, quartettes, or choirs, to sing appropriate selections between the lectures. They may introduce other features for effect, which must in no way alter the proper form of initiation.

When there is a class initiation (over three), to simplify the marching and to save time, the following method may be used. All candidates will proceed to the end of the obligation, when one candidate will be selected to represent the whole in the lectures; the others being seated in the Lodge Room. All will, however, take the charge of the W. P. and the ceremony of Knighthood.

The degree is written as for one candidate, but when there are more than one candidate, the plural form should be used in the proper place.

There are two higher degrees, which were adopted by the Supreme Lodge in session at Cleveland, Ohio, October, 1922, known as the Degree of Patriotism and the Rank of Knighthood. These degrees may be given by following the instructions in the ritual books of these degrees, which can be obtained from the Supreme Secretary.

INITIATORY DEGREE

*(When in the proper order of business, degree work
has been reached, the Worthy President will call the Lodge
to order, and address the Inside Sentinel.)*

W. P.—Worthy Inside Sentinel, ascertain if
any candidate is in waiting for initiation.

*(The Worthy Inside Sentinel inquires through the
Outside Sentinel, and if a candidate is waiting, will report
the name or names of the candidates from his station.)*

W. I. S.—Worthy President, Mr. .... is in
waiting for initiation.

W. P.—Worthy Secretary, has Mr. ....
been constitutionally elected to membership, and
has he paid the required fee?

W. S.—Worthy President, Mr. .... has
been constitutionally elected, and the required fee
has been paid.

W. P.—Worthy Messenger, retire to the outer
room, prepare the candidate in proper form, and
conduct him to the altar of the Lodge.

*(The Worthy Messenger retires in due form, and
after fully preparing the candidate, and in the required
manner, enters the Lodge room with his charge in the
usual form. They march once around the room, and advance
to the altar, while the members sing the Initiation Ode.)*

(Call up.)

INITIATION ODE

(Tune, "Rosseau's Dream")

Enter, Stranger, freely enter;
In our midst no cause for fear:
Each true friend of our dear Order
Meets a hearty welcome here.

Enter, Stranger, freely enter,
None but friends around thee stand,
Off'ring thee, with manly frankness,
Entrance to our noble band.

W. M.—Worthy President, I have brought before you a stranger, who testifies that it is his earnest desire to become a member of our beloved Order. He claims to be of our blood and kin, with the necessary qualifications entitling him to admission. I have therefore brought him before you, that he may join with us in the obligations and privileges of our Order.

W. P.—My Friend, you are now in the presence of those of your own blood and kin; who have pledged themselves to promote peace and good will between the United States and England, and to be just and true in their relations with all mankind, and to give aid to their fellow members in times of sickness and distress. Are you willing to join us, and take unto yourself a like obligation?

Candidate—I am.

W. P.—With this assurance on your part, we will proceed, first calling on our Worthy Chaplain to invoke the Divine Blessing. Brethren, you will give reverent attention to the prayer of the Worthy Chaplain.

W. C.—Let us invoke the blessing of Almighty God upon this candidate.

Prayer

W. C.—O Thou Great and Loving Father, the Creator of the Universe, we approach Thee with reverence and humility. We thank Thee for the manifold blessings Thou has bestowed upon us, and especially for the privilege of meeting together in this brotherhood, banded together for the promotion of each other's welfare and the mitigation of suffering in time of sickness or distress. Look now in tender compassion on this candidate, who now seeks to join with us in this our noble purpose. Give him wisdom and understanding; purge his mind of every selfish and evil desire; may he seek his greatest happiness in doing good to others; strengthen his every noble purpose; and suffer no evil or misfortune to befall him. Seal Thou the consecration he now makes on bended knee at this altar; and may he be ever true to the solemn vows he here may take; and when he has fought the last good fight, may he be found rejoicing with the angelic host in the Heavenly Home of our Father, amidst the joys of reunited Brotherhood. Amen.

(Call down.)

W. P.—My Friend, before you can further advance, it is required that you take a solemn and binding vow; one which I assure you will not deprive you of any liberty that you now or should hereafter enjoy; nor will it embarrass you in the performance of your future duty to God, your country, family or yourself. Do you now cheerfully volunteer to take this vow?

Candidate—I do.

(Call up.)

W. P.—Worthy Messenger, proceed with our friend to the altar, and place him in the required form. The Officers and members will assemble in position around the altar.

(Candidate is caused to kneel on both knees at the altar, right hand resting on the shield and sword, supported by the Holy Bible. The Worthy Messenger stands beside and to the left of the candidate. The Worthy Vice-President directly behind the candidate and Messenger. The Worthy Past President and Chaplain stand on either side of the altar and help form an inner circle, the brethren forming an outer circle around the altar, each with his right hand upon the shoulder of the other, leaving room for the Worthy President to come from his station into the inner circle.)

W. M.—Worthy President, the candidate is in position to take the obligation.

(The Worthy President advances to the inner circle around the altar.)

W. P. —My Friend, you are now in the presence of those who are about to accept you as a Brother. The vows you are about to take are serious and lifelong in duration. Place your right hand on the Bible, sword and shield of St. George; raise your left hand with the index finger pointing upward; and pay strict attention to the vows you are about to make.

(The Worthy Messenger will assist the candidate to place his hands in the proper position.)

W. P.—You will repeat after me: I, in the name of God and St. George, and in the presence of the Brethren here assembled, do solemnly and sincerely promise that, regardless of the circumstances in which I may be placed, I will never reveal any of the signs, grips, passwords, or any of the secret work of this Order. I will keep secret any business of a private nature transacted in this Lodge or any Lodge I may attend. I will faithfully uphold and obey the constitution and laws of the Supreme Lodge, the Grand Lodge of this jurisdiction, and the bylaws of this Lodge; and I will show due respect to all Officers constitutionally installed. I will not speak ill of a Worthy Brother, but will defend his character as I would my own. I will, to the best of my ability, help a Brother in need of assistance, and will exercise my best efforts to promote the welfare of my fellow members. I will be loyal to the established government in the United States of America. (Note: Here substitute Dominion of Canada, in Canadian Lodges.) And I will, with every power at my command, help to maintain peace between the two great families of the English speaking race. I will not discuss sectarian, religious, or partisan political subjects during a session of this Lodge, nor introduce any subject foreign or harmful to the interest of this Order. I make these promises and vows with full knowledge of my responsibility, and will keep this vow inviolate as long as life shall last. So help me God; and may He help me to keep this solemn obligation and be faithful to the promises and vows I here have made.

(Worthy Messenger will remove hoodwinks; all members drop hands to sides, and join in singing the Obligation Ode.)

Obligation Ode.

W. P.—Worthy Messenger, assist the candidate to arise, and conduct him to the station of the Worthy Vice-President for instructions.

(Call down.)

W. M.—Worthy Vice-President, by the direction of the Worthy President, I have the pleasure of presenting to you our newly obligated Brother, who now awaits your instructions.

W. V. P.—My Brother, having made your solemn vows, it is my duty as well as privilege to inform you that the American Order, Sons of St. George, was founded in the year eighteen hundred and seventy, in Scranton, Pennsylvania, primarily for the purpose of enforcing civil law and order, at a time when the regularly constituted authorities for the enforcement of law had suffered a regional lapse, and misguided enmity towards those of English descent had resulted in cowardly and willful murder. A Gideon band of noble souls, from the coal mining district in and around Scranton, responding to the call of humanity, covenanted together, each pledging to the other that, for each innocent life taken in violation of the law, the guilty should be justly punished under the law; pledging themselves also to the restoration of that God-given right of life, liberty and the pursuit of happiness, guaranteed to all alike under the constitution of the United States. From this beginning was evolved a mutual benevolent fraternity, for the administration of financial benefits in sickness; comfort for the dying; the assurance of a be-fitting funeral for the dead; and to encourage the economic, social and intellectual uplift of its members. While the Order is of American origin, one of our important principles is to cultivate the closest friendship, and to do whatever lies within our power, calculated to strengthen the bonds of Brotherhood between the two great families of the Anglo-Saxon race. The Worthy Messenger will now conduct you to the station of the Past Worthy President for further instructions.

W. M.—Past Worthy President, by the direction of the Worthy Vice-President, I present to you our Brother for further instruction.

P. W. P.—My Brother, as you were instructed at the last station, our Order is of American origin. It is therefore fitting that we should foster and cultivate a spirit of true patriotism, a reverence for the memory of our forefathers, and a devotion to the high ideals of our constitution. While enjoying the opportunities and liberties guaranteed to all who live here, we must jealously guard the liberties of others. The history of this country teaches that the Cavaliers of England who settled at Jamestown, Virginia, in the year sixteen hundred and seven, and the English Pilgrims who founded the first colony at Plymouth, Massachusetts, in sixteen hundred and twenty, founded the ideals of a true democracy, out of which grew the United States. The great and illustrious names of those who have been leaders before and since we became a sovereign nation will always embellish the pages of history. Not alone in this country great in its ideals of democracy, but also in science, in art, in literature, in mechanical ingenuity, and invention. But its greatest attribute is its humanitarian principles: offering equal rights and opportunities to all who come under the protection of its flag—the Stars and Stripes. A helpful interest is also taken in all peoples, of any nation, who may need help in times of calamities, of whatever nature. My Brother, these principles of Americanization have been enumerated that you may engender a true feeling of patriotism and pride in this great country.

Worthy Messenger, you will now conduct our Brother to the Worthy Chaplain, for further instruction.

(Note: In place of the foregoing lecture, the following lecture is for use by Lodges of the Order within the Dominion of Canada.)

P. W. P.—My Brother, you were instructed at the last station that the American Order, Sons of St. George, was founded in the United States for the purpose of helping men of English heritage in times of distress. It has since developed into a great fraternity, and while still sustaining the prime objects of its origin, has embraced the further object of cultivating peace and good will between the British Empire and the United States —the two great families of the English speaking world. All worthy sons given by England to the world, wherever found (like the Mother Country herself) have adopted St. George as their patron Saint.

The Order therefore welcomes you because you have like kinship and ideals. The feeling of patriotism and pride you feel in being an integral part of the great Dominion of Canada and the British Empire can the better be fostered and exercised by embracing the principles of our Order.

We are justly proud of the great men and women whose names embellish the history of Canada, and who have assisted in making it one of the brightest jewels in the Empire. Their example of sound government permeates the high standard of civilization of North America. Its emblem, the maple leaf, is a symbol of the highest code of justice, honor, integrity and industry. This has resulted in a feeling of security, peace and harmony between Canada and the United States, and a wonderful example of international good will, unique among nations. Not a fortress or gun has frowned across the frontiers of either nation for over a hundred years. We accept your presence here as a proof of your good intent to uphold, by example as well as by precept, the canons and principles of the society of which you are now a part; and that you will unite with us in spreading the blessings of Anglo-Saxon civilization, to the best of your ability, in the land of your birth, or of which you are now a resident, with honor to yourself and to the Order Sons of St. George.

Worthy Messenger, you will now conduct our Brother to the Worthy Chaplain, for further instruction.

W. M.—Worthy Chaplain, by direction of our Past Worthy President I present to you for further instruction our Brother, who has taken the obligation and received the instruction of the Worthy Vice-President, and that of the Past Worthy President.

W. C.—My Brother, your desire to join us as a Son of St. George, is an indication that your inspirations and ambitions are in sympathy with the best traditions of the Mother Country, and that you seek fraternal communion with us. It is fitting, therefore, that we emulate not only the life of St. George, the patron saint of Old England, but that we exercise in our everyday life those principles which have caused England and the British Empire to be synonomous with honor and obedience to law. You have just cause to be proud of your ancestry. For near a thousand years the flag of St. George has been the emblem of freedom. When King John, in the year twelve hundred and fifteen, at Runnymede, was compelled by free Englishmen to sign the great Magna Charta, true democracy was born, not alone to England, but to the entire world. The great men and women whose names embellish the history of England have been instrumental in advancing the theory of sound government and the highest ethics of those principles which are beneficial to mankind.

My Brother, let me impress upon you the ever growing importance of holding fast to all the great attributes of the English character; so that this great country may never lose the high ideals of the forefathers, always remembering that the people of England and the United States come largely of one common heritage.

Worthy Messenger, you will conduct our Brother to the Worthy President; inform him that he has been instructed at the several stations, and is now well qualified to receive the high honor of Knighthood and such further instruction as only one of his rank can give.

W. M.—Worthy President, I am directed by our Worthy Chaplain to present to you our newly-made Brother. He has been instructed at our several stations, and is well qualified to receive the high Honor of Knight, and such other instruction as only one of your degree can give.

W. P.—My Brother, I congratulate you on your advancement; and it is to be hoped and expected that the lessons already imparted to you will profoundly impress your mind and rightly influence your future conduct. It becomes my duty, as Worthy President of this Lodge, to give you such further instruction as will enable you to properly fulfill the duties you have now assumed by your obligation.

The words used as the motto of our Order are "Fraternity, Concord and Love", the initials of which, "F., C. and L." you may use when addressing a communication to one of your Brethren. This is the grip . . . . Should you wish to make a test to make sure that the man whom you have met is a member of our Order you will . . . . and he will return by . . . . The position of the fingers will always remind you that we are one in heart and hand for the welfare of our Brotherhood. This is the Saluta-

tion Sign .... Placing of the .... thus is intended
to remind you of the obligation we all have taken.
Raising the .... thus, is to impress upon you the
absolute necessity of forever keeping secret all
that takes place in the Lodge Room; and returning
the .... thus, is the open hand of fellowship,
which we offer to all Worthy Brothers. This ....
is the salute to be given in honor of a visit by a
Grand Lodge Officer (when announced as such).
This .... is the salute in honor of a visit by a Supreme Lodge Officer (when announced as such).
This .... is the voting sign.

I will instruct you how to gain admittance to
a Lodge of this Order. If the Lodge is not in session, you will clothe yourself in proper regalia,
enter the room and take your seat. If the Lodge is
in session, you will approach the outer door and give
such an alarm as will attract the attention of the
Outside Sentinel. He will raise the wicket and you
will give him the first half of the current password,
which is .... You will then be admitted to the
ante-room, where you will clothe yourself in proper
regalia, advance to the inner door, where you will
.... If your alarm is returned, you will know
there is business before the Lodge, and must await
its conclusion. When the wicket is raised by the
Inside Sentinel, you will give your name, and the
name and number of your Lodge, in this way:
Brother .... of .... Lodge No. ....., (that being
the name and number of this Lodge). You will
also give the second half of the password, which
is .... You will then be admitted, and must at
once proceed to the front of the altar, facing the

Worthy President, and salute by giving the Salutation Sign . . . ., which the Worthy President will return, when you may be seated. Should you forget the Password, you will so report to the Sentinels, and upon being admitted you will salute the Worthy President; and, before taking your seat, present yourself at the station of the Past Worthy President, who will give you the password if you are entitled to receive it. Should you wish to retire while the Lodge is in session, you will approach the altar and give the Salutation Sign . . . .; and if returned by the Worthy President you may retire.

I will now explain to you the use of the gavel. . . . . commands order in the Lodge room and seats the Lodge when standing: . . . . the officers will rise: . . . . the entire Lodge will rise.

(All members rise.)

W. P.—Worthy Messenger, you will place the Brother in position to receive the high Honor of Knighthood.

(The Worthy Messenger assists the Brother to kneel on right knee on stool or platform, the Worthy President, with sword in hand, steps in front of the Brother and says:)

W. P.—By virtue of the trust reposed and power vested in me by my Brother Knights, I now invest you with the degree of Knighthood, and with this good sword I dub thee Knight; in the name of God (taps Brother with sword over left shoulder), our country (taps again) and St. George (taps). Rise, Brother Knight, and may you prove to be true and worthy.

W. P.—I will now decorate your breast with the badge of our Order, which should be hereafter worn by you during Lodge session only; unless otherwise directed by the Worthy President.

W. P.—This badge when on your breast is a symbol of your membership within the Order; likewise of your devotion to its principles and teachings. It is also an outward sign of your inward pledge that, as far as in you lies, you will keep pure the channels of your thoughts as required in the motto, thereon inscribed, "Honi Soit Qui Mal Y Pense",—the English translation of which is, "Evil be to him who evil thinks". Worthy Messenger, you will present our Brother to the Worthy Chaplain, who will give him the closing words of advice and instruction.

W. M.—Worthy Chaplain, I am directed by our Worthy President to present this Brother, who has just received the high Honor of Knighthood, for final advice and counsel, which you are well qualified to impart.

W. C.—My Brother, I will now present you with this official button, bearing the imprint of the emblem of our Order; as the Knights of old wore on their armor the insignia of their Knightly vows, we trust you will wear this emblem as the insignia of your Knightly vows; and may its presence ever inspire you to attain every Knightly virtue. In closing, My Brother, let me remind you that the motto of our Order is the three words, "Fraternity, Concord and Love". Fraternity has a meaning stronger and more beautiful in its relative value than friendship: it is the uniting of men in the bonds of Brotherly interest. While Concord means union, there can be no Concord unless there be Fraternity. These two virtues are interblended. The last of the trio of words cherished by our Order is Love: it is the greatest and best of all virtues. Fraternity and Concord without Love are void and without meaning. The unseen power which rules and regulates the highest human impulses is Love.

My Brother, we sincerely hope that the solemn vows you have taken will be to you no idle ceremony, to be forgotten as a passing dream, but a pleasant reality of manly duties assumed. Longfellow tells us in one of his poems that

> "Life is real, life is earnest,
>   And the grave is not its goal;
> Dust thou art, to dust returnest,
>   Was not written of the soul.
>
> "Not enjoyment and not sorrow
>   Is our destined end or way;
> But to act that each tomorrow
>   Finds us farther than today."

Worthy Messenger, you will conduct our Brother to the Worthy Secretary, that he may sign our constitution; then proceed to the Worthy President.

W. M.—Worthy President, the Brother in my charge has received the closing instruction from our Worthy Chaplain, and now awaits your commands.

W. P.—(Taking newly-made Brother by the right hand.) My Brother, in behalf of our beloved Order, and for myself, I welcome you into the fellowship of . . . . Lodge, No. . . . . ., whose sacred words, "Fraternity, Concord and Love" should cause you to become stronger and firmer in the ties of Brotherhood and the advancement of our Order. Worthy Messenger, you will place our Brother in position at the altar to receive the grip of welcome from the Brethren here assembled.

W. P.—Officers and Brothers, I have the pleasure of introducing Brother . . . . I commend him to your good offices. Let us give him the grip.

WELCOME ODE

Here's the grip; Brother take it;
*   'Tis a Freeman's true grasp,*
With the pledge of his honor
*   As thy hand he doth clasp.*
'Tis the promise he gives thee
*   That, true to his creed,*
He will help a true Brother,
*   In the time of his need.*

Here's the grip; Brother take it;
*   'Tis a Patriot's true sign*
That his heart goes out with it
*   To mingle with thine.*
Then take, and return it,
*   Wherever you be,*
To each Son of St. George
*   That may give it to thee.*

(When all have returned to their stations, the Worthy President will say:)

W. P.—Worthy Messenger, you will escort our Brother to a seat in the room.

(Call down.)

(Business may be resumed or a recess may be declared to welcome the newly-made Brother.)

INSTALLATION OF OFFICERS

(Elected or Appointed)

This Ceremony may be made public if desired, omitting all signs, etc.

(The Grand President and Grand Messenger [or Deputies] will visit the Lodge on the night of installation, and at the proper time retire to the ante-room, when the Grand Messenger will enter the Lodge Room and after saluting at the Altar will say:)

G. M.—Worthy President, the Grand President (or Deputy Grand President) is in the ante-room awaiting your pleasure to install the Officers of this Lodge for the coming term, and as a warrant of his authority, I will read his commission.

(Reads commission.)

W. P.—Grand Messenger, you will kindly retire; inform the Grand President that we are ready for installation and await his presence.

(The Grand Messenger retires and escorts the Grand President into Lodge Room, both saluting at Altar. As they enter the Worthy President will)

(Call up.)

(While at the Altar the Grand Messenger will say:)

G. M.—Worthy President, I have the honor to present to this Lodge Grand President (or Deputy) . . . ., who is here to install your Officers for the coming term.

W. P.—Grand President, I cordially invite you to a seat on my right.

W. P.—Officers and Brothers, let us honor our Grand Lodge Officers with the Grand Lodge salute taking time from our Worthy Messenger.

(Call down.)

G. P. (or Deputy).—Worthy President, I hold in my hand my commission giving me power and authority to have general supervision over this Lodge and to install your officers. I shall therefore proceed with the installation.

Worthy President, have the Officers to be installed been constitutionally elected or appointed?

W. P.—They have.

G. P.—Are they in good standing and free from charges?

W. P.—They are in good standing and free from charges.

G. P.—Worthy President, by the authority given me by the Grand Lodge of this Jurisdiction, I must request you to deliver into my care, the charter, rituals, books and gavel, that I may place them in the care of your successor. Your work, however, is not done. You have performed the duties connected with your office to the best of your ability. The experience you have gained is valuable to your Lodge, and you will be expected to continue your interest, by doing all in your power to further the welfare of this Lodge and the Order in general. Be punctual in your attendance, and let the honored title of Past Worthy

President which you have so justly earned, be to you no hollow sounding title.

W. P.—Grand President, before surrendering my gavel and the properties of this Lodge, now in my possession to you, it is my pleasant duty to thank the officers and members of this Lodge for the many kindnesses and courtesies extended to me while occupying this chair, believing that my term of service has not lessened the confidence and respect reposed in me when you so kindly elected me as Presiding Officer of this Lodge.

Grand President, unto your hands I give the gavel, books and charter, hoping my successor whom you are about to install will be blessed with health and strength to faithfully perform the duties of his office, and that the Lodge will prosper under his administration.

(The Worthy President now takes a seat on the right of the Grand President.)

G. P.—Worthy Secretary, please favor me with a list of the Officers elected or appointed.

The Officers for the term now ending will please vacate their chairs and surrender to the Grand Messenger their Regalia and all Lodge property now in their possession.

(When the Officers vacate their chairs, they will advance to the Grand Messenger who stands in front of, but three paces back from, the Altar, to receive their Regalia. Having collected the Regalia, the Grand Messenger returns to his station and the Grand President will call up and say:)

G. P.—Worthy President, you will now please take your seat as Junior Past Worthy President.

Grand Messenger conduct the Past Worthy President to his chair.

(Call down.)

Grand Messenger conduct the Worthy President, Vice-President and Messenger-Elect to the ante-room, examine them as to their qualifications for the offices to which they have been elected and be sure they understand thoroughly the secret work of our Order.

(The Grand Messenger and Officers-Elect as named, salute, retire and after examination will return, salute and the G. M. will report if he finds them correct as follows:)

G. M.—Grand President, I have examined the Officers-Elect and found them qualified and well versed in the secret work of our Order.

G. P.—Grand Messenger, place the Officers-Elect and appointed in position in front of the dais, the Worthy President at my right and the others according to their rank.

(When all are standing before the Grand President, he will say:)

G. P.—My Brothers, the duties connected with the office of Worthy President, Worthy Vice-President, Worthy Secretary, Worthy Treasurer, Worthy Messenger, Worthy Assistant Secretary and Worthy Trustee, are plainly and forcibly laid down for your guidance in the subordinate lodge Constitution. You will be expected to study and learn your duties as directed therein.

The Worthy Assistant Messenger shall assist the Worthy Messenger in opening and closing the Lodge and such other duties as are laid down in the Grand Lodge Constitution and By-Laws of this Lodge.

The Worthy Chaplain's duties are of a reverential nature. His duties require him to assist in such ceremonies as are required of him by the Ritual.

The Worthy Inside Sentinel shall have charge of the inner door. It is his duty to prove every Brother, and announce his name to the Past Worthy President and obtain his permission before admitting him. He must see that all Brothers have on their Regalia.

The Worthy Outside Sentinel's, duties are in the ante-room. Upon the strict and faithful performance of his duties depends the privacy of the Lodge. He will see that no person enters who cannot prove himself according to the rules and regulations of our Order. He must keep the outer door secure against improper intrusion and submit all cases where he has a doubt to the Worthy Inside Sentinel to be reported to the Worthy President for his action.

Having been instructed in your several duties, do you each accept the office to which you have been elected?

Answer—I do.

G. P.—'Tis well.

(Call up.)

Place your right hand on your left breast, raise your left hand with the index finger pointing upwards, and repeat after me:

I do solemnly promise to perform the duties of the office to which I have been elected, as laid down in the Constitution and Laws of the American Order, Sons of St. George, and the By-Laws of this Lodge, to the best of my ability, and to do all in my power, by punctual attendance at our regular meetings, to promote the best interests of this Lodge and the Order in general. I make this pledge upon my honor as a Son of St. George.

(Sing OBLIGATION ODE.)

G. P.—Grand Messenger, invest them with the badges of their offices and conduct them to their several stations. The Trustee to a seat in the body of the Lodge first and the others according to their office.

(The Grand Messenger will conduct all the officers to their stations. The Worthy President on the left of the Grand President. The Grand President will then turn to the Worthy President and deliver the following charge.)

G. P.—Worthy President, before I deliver into your keeping the charter and books pertaining to your office, it becomes my duty to call your attention to a promise you made when entering this Order, namely, that you must avoid reading or rehearsing any part of the work of this Order before or in the hearing of any person not a member. You must not print or write, or allow to be printed or written, any of the secret work of our Order. Keep the Rituals in your own care, and deliver these books to none but a Grand Lodge Officer or Deputy.

Having full confidence in your integrity, I now present you with the Charter, Books, copy of the Laws of the Order, and lastly the Gavel, the symbol of your authority, and heartily greet you (here shakes hands) as Worthy President of . . . . Lodge, No. . . . . . and hope you may have health and strength to fill the important position you now occupy.

Brethren of . . . . Lodge, No. . . . . ., American Order, Sons of St. George, I . . . . . . by the powers vested in me by the Grand Lodge of our beloved Order, do declare the Officers of . . . . Lodge, No. . . . . duly and legally installed for the term.

(The Worthy President may resume business or declare a recess. If it is a public installation, the regular Lodge business must be done previous to the ceremony.)

(Call down.)

VISITATIONS

(When a Supreme Lodge Officer, Grand Lodge Officer, or visiting Brothers in a body announce themselves to the Worthy Inside Sentinel, he will report the same to the Worthy President, who shall appoint a committee of one or more to retire and introduce them. On the entrance of the visitors the Worthy President will)

(Call up.)

(After the Salutation and while the visiting Brothers stand at the Altar the Worthy President will say:)

W. P.—In the name of this Lodge, permit me to tender you a hearty welcome, and to hope that your visit may prove a pleasure to you, and a profit to us.

W. P.—Officers and Brothers, I take great
pleasure in introducing to you . . . . . .

We will now honor him with the Supreme (or
Grand Lodge) salute, taking time from our
Worthy Messenger.

(All salute.)

W. P.—And now Supreme (or Grand) . . . .
permit me to resign into your hand the gavel of
this Lodge.

*(The visitor will accept the gavel and after a few
appropriate remarks, will return it to the Worthy President, who will continue the business of the Lodge.)*

(Call down.)

FORM OF INSTITUTING NEW LODGES

*(The instituting officers and staff will take their sta-
tions, as in the opening of a Subordinate Lodge, request all
the applicants for Charter who are not members of the
Order to retire, and then open in usual form; after the
Charter members are initiated, the instituting officer will
say:)*

G. P.—Brethren, we are assembled here to fulfill an interesting and pleasing duty, that of creat-
ing a new branch of our beloved Order, and I hope
and trust that you will find association with us to
be of such great advantage socially, morally and

materially, that you will never have cause to regret having joined this Order; but, on the contrary, will be so well pleased as to lose no opportunity to induce others to follow you, and thus strengthen and extend our aims, objects and good influences. Although it should be the aim of every Lodge to increase its membership, let me impress upon you to be very careful in introducing individuals for membership in our beloved Order, of whom you, in your inward heart, have a doubt. In fact, your best guide is, to recommend no man whom you will not be willing afterward to welcome in your own home, and introduce to your family. New Lodges are inclined to be a little careless in this matter, but it should not be so. One unworthy man admitted to membership may cause you to lose many who would have made desirable members and been a benefit to your Lodge. And to you who may hereafter, or perhaps tonight, be appointed on investigating committees, I would say, it is your duty, not so much to visit the candidate, although this is requisite, as it is to thoroughly inquire into his mode of life, and general reputation for probity, morality and respectability.

And now, my Brethren, let me advise you that in all your discussions and differences of opinion, which you are sure to have, that you never forget to treat each other with due respect. We all have ideas of our own, and it is only manly to express them, but in so doing, let us avoid all sarcasm, irony, personalities, and ungenerous remarks, and when beaten fairly, give graciously in, always remembering that one or the other must lose his point.

I will now call upon the Grand Secretary to read the Charter, under which you will have the pleasure of working so long as you comply with its requirements and the laws of our Order.

(G. S. reads Charter.)

And now, Brethren, before you elect your officers, I would charge you to elect, as officers of this Lodge, none but those you believe to be thoroughly competent to fill the same, and let no one accept either a position as an officer, or on a committee, unless you feel that you are competent, and have the necessary time to discharge the duties of the same. Ambition is laudable, aim high and you certainly will not strike low; do whatever you have to do thoroughly well, rest on your merits, and your success is certain; and, lastly, let me impress you with the fact that, to be successful, you must always bow to the will of the majority; follow this, you will be prosperous, and harmony your constant guest. I now declare nomination and election of officers in order.

(At conclusion of which, install, as per regular ceremony, and then say:)

Officers and Brothers, by the authority in me vested as . . . . I declare . . . . Lodge, No. . . . . . duly and legally instituted a Lodge of the American Order, Sons of St. George.

FUNERAL CEREMONY

The Worthy President will make arrangements for the members (or a delegation) to meet punctually at the time called, either at the Lodge room or some other suitable place.

Enough sprigs of evergreen should be provided so that every member may wear a sprig in the lapel of his coat. Dark clothes should be worn as far as possible, white gloves and funeral badges.

The members having assembled, the Worthy President will act as Marshal, or appoint some other Brother in his place.

The Members will form in procession, two by two, preceded by the Officers in the following order.

First—Supreme and Grand Lodge Officers.
Second—Past Presidents.
Third—Officers of the Lodge.
Fourth—Members.

On arrival at the home of the deceased Brother, the Members will open ranks, and permit the body to be carried through to the hearse, after which they will march to the front of the hearse, Members, Officers, Past Presidents. Grand and Supreme Officers last. Upon arriving at the church, or cemetery, ranks are broken and the body and mourners pass through the ranks. Then the Officers and Members will follow in due form.

Arriving at the grave the Worthy President will stand at the head, and the Worthy Chaplain at the foot, the Officers and Members around the grave in as good order as the nature of the ground will admit. (Should the services be conducted at the home of the deceased Brother, the Worthy President and Worthy Chaplain will stand as near the coffin as possible, while delivering the service.)

After the regular religious ceremony, and before closing the grave, the Worthy President will deliver his address, followed by the prayer of the Worthy Chaplain.

W. P.—Brethren and Friends: We are assembled to render the last office the living may minister to the dead, the last act we perform for a departed Brother. We do not assemble to benefit the deceased, but rather to impress upon the minds of surviving friends, the necessity of preparing to meet the summons, when it shall be our turn to cancel the debt we owe to nature. "Man is born to die." The decree of Heaven is, "Dust thou art, and unto dust thou shalt return." We must all wait the inevitable hour. What is our life? "It is even a vapor that appeareth for a little time, and then vanisheth away." Where are the myriads of the human family who have lived and figured on the earth? "They are asleep with their fathers, and the place that once knew them, shall know them no more forever."

Oh, let us, then, reflect and be prepared for the change which awaits us all. Death comes when least expected, and spares none. He calls for youth in its harmlessness and innocency, manhood in its vigor and prime, and old age, tottering and decrepit. My brethren, we are too easily dazzled with the pursuits, pleasures and wealth of this world. Although hardly a day passes but we see or hear of disaster, accident or death, yet how seldom do we think of our own mortality. Often we are called upon to follow our fellow-men to the grave, yet we immediately return to the world, heedless, perhaps, of the precarious tenure of life, and the uncertainty of that end to which all flesh is rapidly tending; the living of today may be the dead of tomorrow, "for we appear and disappear like the waves of the sea." "In the midst of life we are in death." Death is no respecter of persons; all must bow, rich and poor, weak and strong, the lowest beggar and the king on the throne—all are leveled by Death.

Brethren, let us, then, not fix our minds on worldly things, which we cannot stay to enjoy, but let us be concerned in erecting for ourselves a mansion where time loses its power, and enjoyment will be eternal. It is sad, very sad, for a man to so give his time to self in this world, as to miss the way to his best and most lasting home in the future.

Finally, Brethren, let us forget the faults of our deceased Brother, and keep alive in our memory, only his many virtues and noble actions; let us profit by the good example he gave us while living, and keep his memory forever green. May this loss of a Brother, impress us with the necessity of so conducting our own lives, that when it shall be our turn to leave this world, we may die feeling at peace, with all mankind and our Maker

W. C.—Let us pray :

O merciful and adorable God, who art the Resurrection and the Life, in whom all shall live who believeth in Thee, though they die; hear, we beseech Thee, the prayers of these Thy servants assembled for the purpose of committing to the earth the remains of our late Brother, whom Thou, in Thy divine wisdom, hast removed from our midst. Give us, O God, whom Thou hast spared, a full knowledge of our helplessness and dependence upon Thee, that we may meditate upon our own mortality, and cease to neglect the many opportunities of improvement in our lives which Thy goodness hath graciously afforded. Impress upon all present the uncertainty of life, and the certainty of death. Look down, O God, bless and comfort the disconsolate family, give them strength to bear up under this great affliction, sustain them in their desponding moments, and so imbue their hearts with a spirit of resignation, that they may be able to say: "Not my will, but Thine, O Lord, be done." Bless this Brotherhood, impress each with their duty to the other, give to our bodies health, and refresh our souls with the remembrance of Thee—the Bread of Life and the Fountain of every good.—Amen.

W. P.—The Brothers will now join in singing the FUNERAL ODE on Page 53:

(If only a small number of members are present the FUNERAL ODE may be omitted.)

At the conclusion of the ceremony the Officers and members will drop their piece of evergreen into the grave saying as they do so IN MEMORY.

The Brothers may be dismissed or march back to the place of assembly as the Marshal may direct.

It is the duty of the Worthy Messenger to collect all Lodge property.

Funeral Ode.

Tune, "Hanover."

REGALIA OF THE ORDER

MEMBERS

"The Knights of the Garter" Badge is a metal medallion 1¾ inches in diameter, comprising:

(a) An encircling garter in blue enamel 3-16 inches in width, bearing motto in raised gold letters ⅛-inch in height, "Honi Soit Qui Mal Y Pense." Buckle of Garter located ½-inch left of bottom of design. Eyelet end of garter looped over at bottom; garter from buckle to end pierced with buckle holes.

(b) Within the encircling garter a relief figure in gold of St. George and the Dragon. St. George mounted on horseback facing right; nude except for cloak streaming from neck; carrying short Roman sword drawn to thrust. Dragon prone under feet of horse, head upraised between front feet of horse.

The medallion suspended by chains from a bar 1 15-16 inches long lettered in relief with the word "Member." Bar fitted with hard solder joint and catch No. 16 B. & S. pin.

SUBORDINATE LODGES

An upper bar two inches long lettered in relief "A. O. S. St. G." Second bar lettered with abbreviation of proper official title. A medallion similar to medallion described in the Member's Badge. Bars and medallion connected by chains. The upper bar supporting the appropriate emblem of office and fitted with No. 16 B. & S. pin.

A set of officers' badges shall consist of fourteen, which with the appropriate emblems of office, are as follows:

Junior P. P.	A star
W. President	Crossed Gavels
W. V. President	Single gavel
W. Secretary	Crossed quills
W. Treasurer	Crossed keys
W. Messenger	Dove carrying olive twig in bill
W. Chaplain	Open Bible
W. Asst. Secretary	Single quill
W. Asst. Messenger	Same as Messenger
W. Inside Sentinel	Crossed swords
W. Outside Sentinel	Single sword
W. Trustee (3)	Padlock with key on it

PAST PRESIDENTS

A medallion comprising the garter 1⅛ inches in diameter, blue enamel, with motto, "Honi Soit Qui Mal Y Pense," enclosing St. George and Dragon. Background cut out. Foliations or ornament of conventional design surrounding the garter so that the full diameter of medallion shall be 1 9-16 inches. Suspend medallion from bar 1¾ inches long lettered in relief "P. W. P." by two chains 1⅛ inches long. From bar suspended in center a five-pointed star in blue enamel 7-16 inches in length. Add cross gavels 1 8-16 inches rigidly attached at top of medallion. Finished in three grades. A. 1-10 14-karat gold. B. 1-10 10-karat gold. C. Roman gold. Each badge enclosed in first quality standard watergrain leather badge case.

DISTRICT DEPUTY GRAND PRESIDENTS

A red enamel vertical cross with superimposed medallion as above described. Blue enamel star as in next following. Encircle garter with band same width as garter passing over the lateral and lower arms and cut away or appearing to pass under the upper arm. "Deputy Grand President" lettered in relief upon this band. Extend lower vertical arm of cross so as to expose area of red equal with upper arm.

GRAND LODGE OFFICERS' BADGES

A cross of red enamel $2\frac{5}{8}$ inches by $2\frac{5}{8}$ inches. Width of arms $\frac{3}{4}$ inch. Medallion $1\frac{1}{8}$ inches in diameter, comprising garter, motto, George and Dragon substantially as in members badge above. Upon upper arm of cross blue enamel five-pointed star $\frac{5}{8}$ inches in measure, single point at top, lower points attached to periphery of garter. Upon lower arm of cross suitable insignia of office. Both star and insignia to be pinned to cross. Finished in heavy 18-karat gold plate upon gilding metal, stamped to indicate material and finish. Supported by pin and catch as above described.

PAST GRAND PRESIDENT'S BADGE

A five-pointed star of blue enamel, extreme dimensions 2¼ inches. Gold George and Dragon in center of star. Garter 1¾ inches in diameter surrounding George superimposed on arms of star. Two decorated bars connected at each extremity by chain of three links. From lower bar suspended by two sets of three links a pair of crossed gavels (the point of intersection touching the upper point of star), the hammer faces rigidly attached to periphery of garter. Supporting chains extending from connection with gavel handles to connection with periphery of garter. Engrave upper bar "Past Grand President," lower bar, "A. O. S. St. G." Reverse of star "Presented to   by   Grand Lodge at   year   ." Top bar 2 inches, second bar 1 9-16 inches. Execute in 14-karat gold 15 dwt. fit with safety catch. Top bar with 11 and second bar with 14 piercings. Rider pinned to star and star pinned to garter. Enclosed in first quality standard water-grain leather badge-case.

PAST SUPREME PRESIDENT'S JEWEL

To be identical in general design with Past Grand President's Jewel as above described but substitute star of purple enamel. Top bar 2 inches, second bar 1 7-16 inches. Garter 1¾ inches. Star 2¼ inches. Executed in 14-karat gold 25 dwts. Jewel pinned as in Past Grand President's jewel above described. Deliver in first class standard water-grain leather badge case. Engrave upper bar "Past Supreme President;" lower bar "A. O. S. St. G." On reverse of star "Presented to   by Supreme Lodge, A. O. S. St. G., at   year."

FUNERAL BADGE

Black rosette 3 inches in diameter with black and white button, 1¾ inches in diameter, in centre. Black ribbon 2½ inches wide and 5 inches long from rosette to fringe. Double silver fringe 1½ inches long. Name and number of lodge and St. George and Dragon printed in silver.